All about LIBRARIANS

Brianna Kaiser

Lerner Publications ◆ Minneapolis

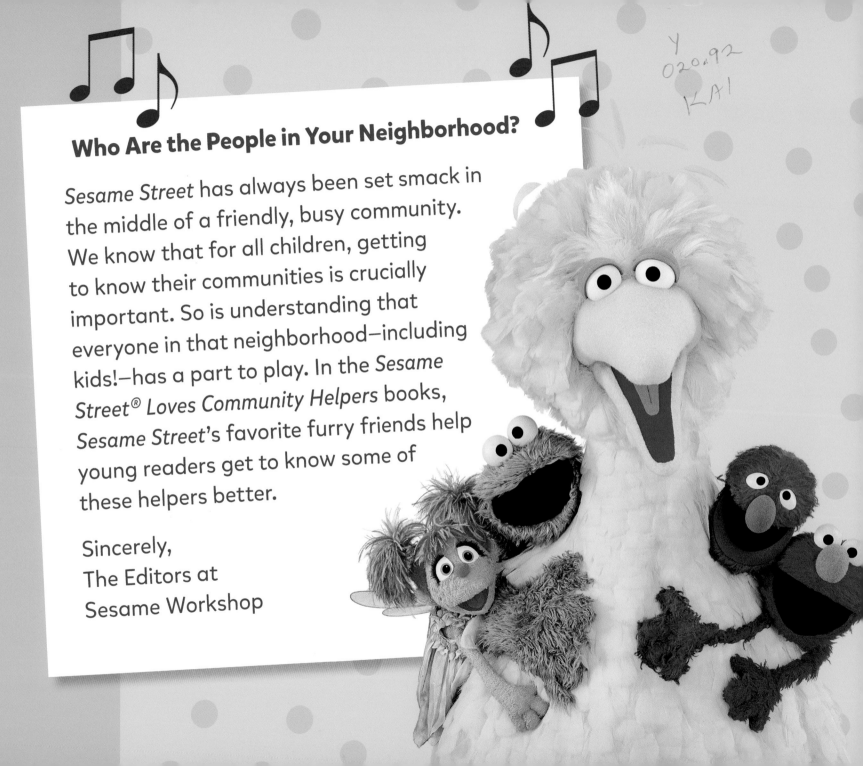

Who Are the People in Your Neighborhood?

Sesame Street has always been set smack in the middle of a friendly, busy community. We know that for all children, getting to know their communities is crucially important. So is understanding that everyone in that neighborhood—including kids!—has a part to play. In the *Sesame Street® Loves Community Helpers* books, *Sesame Street*'s favorite furry friends help young readers get to know some of these helpers better.

Sincerely,
The Editors at
Sesame Workshop

Table of Contents

We Love Librarians!

Librarians are great! They help Elmo find and check out books.

Learn about Librarians

Librarians are community helpers. They help people find books and information.

My librarian helped me learn more about different kinds of bird nests.

They work in libraries. Libraries are places where people can check out books, use computers, and more.

9

Librarians help sign people up for library cards.

People use library cards to borrow books, movies, music, and more.

I love my library card!

When people return books to the library, librarians sort the books.

13

Each library book
has a number.

Librarians put the books on shelves in order by number.

Librarians teach people how to find information in books, e-books, and online.

Librarian help me find cookie recipe.

17

Some librarians work at school libraries. They help students learn about different subjects.

I study animals and plants at school!

Some librarians work in public libraries. These are libraries that are in your neighborhood.

Librarians know when new books are coming out.
They find books that people will like to read.

My favorite books are about geckos.

They also read books at story time.

I like going to the library for story time with my cousin Tamir.

Librarians are always ready to help people. How does your librarian help you?

My librarian helped me learn more about pigeons.

26

Mine helped me find a book on rubber duckies!

Thank You, Librarians!

Now it's your turn! Write a thank-you note to your librarian.

Dear Librarian,

Thank you for helping Elmo learn. Elmo likes coming to the library to find books and go to story time.

Your friend,

Elmo

Picture Glossary

community: a place where people live and work

information: facts or details about something

library card: a card that lets you borrow books and more from the library

study: to look for information

Read More

Moening, Kate. *Librarians*. Minneapolis: Bellwether Media, 2019.

Peterson, Christy. *A Trip to the Library with Sesame Street.* Minneapolis: Lerner Publications, 2022.

Waxman, Laura Hamilton. *Librarian Tools*. Minneapolis: Lerner Publications, 2020.

Index

Photo Acknowledgments

Image credits: SDI Productions/E+/Getty Images, pp. 5, 9, 16; kali9/Getty Images, pp. 6, 27; Mark Edward Atkinson/Getty Images, pp. 7, 30 (top left); Shannon Ramos/EyeEm/Getty Images, p. 8; SW Productions/Getty Images, pp. 10, 30 (bottom left); Shalom Ormsby Images Inc/Getty Images, p. 11; Andersen Ross Photography Inc/Getty Images, p. 12; Hill Street Studios/Getty Images, p. 13; Todd Strand/Independent Picture Service, p. 14; airdone/Shutterstock.com, p. 15; Marc Romanelli/Getty Images, pp. 17, 30 (top right); FatCamera/Getty Images, p. 18; Alex Liew/Getty Images, pp. 19, 30 (bottom right); Marc Romanelli/Getty Images, p. 20; Kevin Wheal/Alamy Stock Photo, p. 21; SeventyFour/Shutterstock.com, p. 22; GoodLifeStudio/Getty Images, p. 23; Digital Vision/Getty Images, p. 24; JGI/Jamie Grill/Getty Images, p. 26; Tyler Olson/Shutterstock.com, p. 29.

Cover: kali9/E+/Getty Images.

Lerner Publications Company
An imprint of Lerner Publishing Group, Inc.
241 First Avenue North
Minneapolis, MN 55401 USA

For reading levels and more information, look up this title at www.lernerbooks.com.

Main body text set in Mikado Medium.
Typeface provided by HVD Fonts.

Editor: Rebecca Higgins **Designer:** Emily Harris
Lerner team: Martha Kranes

Library of Congress Cataloging-in-Publication Data

Names: Kaiser, Brianna, 1996– author.
Title: All about librarians / Brianna Kaiser.
Description: Minneapolis : Lerner Publications, [2023] | Series: Sesame Street loves community helpers | Includes bibliographical references and index. | Audience: Ages 4–8. | Audience: Grades K–1. | Summary: "Join Sesame Street characters to learn all about librarians. Librarians help people find information, check out books, and much more! This accessible approach shows how essential librarians are to every community"– Provided by publisher.
Identifiers: LCCN 2021035572 | ISBN 9781728456102 (library binding) | ISBN 9781728462134 (ebook)
Subjects: LCSH: Librarians–Juvenile literature. | Libraries–Juvenile literature.
Classification: LCC Z682 .K15 2023 | DDC 020.92–dc23

LC record available at https://lccn.loc.gov/2021035572

Manufactured in the United States of America
1-50680-50099-12/1/2021